DID THE BUDDHA HURRY?

WRITINGS TO HELP YOU SLOW DOWN, GAIN PERSPECTIVE, AND FIND INNER WISDOM

KRISTIN KESKEY

KRISTIN KESKEY

Copyright © 2023 by KRISTIN KESKEY

All rights reserved.

No part of this book may be reproduced in any form or by any electronic or mechanical means, including information storage and retrieval systems, without written permission from the author, except for the use of brief quotations in a book review.

CONTENTS

Inspired Art	v
Introduction	vii
Prologue	1
On the Edge of the Sea	3
Clam Chowder	5
Never the Same	7
The Heavy Weight	9
Courage Stew	11
Cold Feet	13
Lesson 101	15
Friend	17
Leap of Faith	19
Spitting Image	21
The Gift	23
Bomb Cyclone	25
Kupuna	27
It's a Shame	29
The Succulent	31
Charging Station	33
Chatterbox	35
The Wedding	37
Yin Yang	39
Molecular	41
Truth Serum	43
Birthday	45
Liar, Liar	47
Haleakala	49
The Hereafter	51
Forest Tree	53
Who?	54
I Hate You	56
Eclipse Returned	58

The Climber's Dilemma	60
Stoney Creek	62
Finally	64
Gen?	66
Suspended Animation	68
The Longest Day of the Year	70
Dog Daze	72
What was I thinking?	75
The Gold Digger	77
The Midnight Sun	79
Aleksanteri	81
Aleksanteri Revisted	83
Metsa (Finnish for Forest)	85
We Used To	87
Really?	89
Super Blue Moon	91
Sleeping In	93
Toenail Moon	95
Just a few questions to keep in mind	97
Dedication	99
Also by KRISTIN KESKEY	101
About the Author	103
About the Author	105

INSPIRED ART

Illustrations and cover drawings by Kristin Keskey

INTRODUCTION

You are embarking on a highly emotional adventure of confronting the depths of change, fear and beauty. Facing unexpected physical challenges, and being inspired by the healing power of nature around us, I have poured my heart into sharing my personal journey and deepest thoughts in the hope that you can see the me that is also you. Take a breath or two, step back, nature can't be rushed, and dive into the ocean of our consciousness.

PROLOGUE

Sharing some thoughts from the author.

Recipes for survival

We don't come with a recipe, blueprint or instructions. Somewhere along the way if we don't have a grandfather or a sugar someone, we have to figure it out. Our story then becomes a roadmap for those fellow unfortunates who also need a little push to stay on the track and not veer over the cliff, or at least not as often. The road map becomes a suit of armor for us, keeping us on the treacherous path of human destiny. Choices, that's what the map shows. This way the quicksand, that way the volcano, or the one foot in front of another hard uphill. After the brutal climb we can sit at the top and see the beautiful vistas spread out, the paths we struggled on. There is no more weariness, just peace, the pat on the back, and then that long trek back down to home. I'm sharing my recipes and roadmaps so your journey might be a bit easier.

Fighting for courage

You never felt brave, only a big hollow where your stomach was. But after the big hard thing, you know, you just know, you were really brave. A feeling of joy rises up. You did it, and now it's behind you. You can skip and jump and smile. It was bad, but now it's over. Like everything else in life, it never lasts long.

Think of your past, your memories. Do they comfort you or haunt you? Or some of both? Think of the close ones who have gone. Their lives roll over you like people in a distant land with no internet. But yet you feel their presence pushing against you. We can imagine the future, but we never imagine the bumps and scrapes that come, or the hard changes we have to confront.

Yet they do come, and with it a great deal of learning. I hope my path with its roadblocks and detours will inspire the best in you.

Writing in the dark

It looks as if I'm going to have to write about writing again. Not about editing or making a pdf or any of those feisty things. Just the pure bliss of having words come into your mind like a plane flying a banner, a really long banner. You can't make this up. You can't imagine it. It just happens.

Turn the page and see what came out.

ON THE EDGE OF THE SEA

Time
  Was the salt water taffy
  In my hands.
Pulled long,
Twisted,
And pulled long,
Again.
Finally,
The sky
Went from soft orange
To velvet black.
On the horizon,
The glow
Of a distant
Unseen island.
It hovers,
Mysterious.
Real or unreal?
The stars prickle
Boldly,

And don't disappear.
Unlike the distant nebulae
Seen only
With the side-ways
Glance.
Did I see that?
The thrill of the cosmos,
The sense
Of the tipsy earth,
Viewing
While spinning and wobbling,
The rest of the universe.
Turning with it,
Slowing for a moment,
To feel the night
Treasure,
Holding me
In its dark arms,
Rocking me into
Dreamtime,
Safe in the knowing
The taffy will pull me
Into the pink, cloudy
Dawn,
And the hot feel
Of awake,
The bird-song
Of everything
All over again.

CLAM CHOWDER

There is a clam
    Within the heart
      Of me.
I am desperately
Digging it out.
Shovel sand
And it resists,
Diving deeper.
The sea,
Complicit in it's burial,
Sealed,
But alive,
Not revealed.
So precious
Only to me.
Cast aside,
Or too ugly
Would be heartbreaking.

. . .

Smooth over the sand.
    Let it live
    Beneath,
    In it's own beauty,
    Perhaps,
    One day,
    A wise one
    Will dig
    Until exhausted
    To find the treasure deep,
    Meant to be
    Held close
    And not
    Rejected.

NEVER THE SAME

In the soft, warm,
    Comforting air,
    The breeze
Moist,
And caressing
Feels perfect.
You crave it
To continue.

In the cold,
    Shivery,
    Snow pelting,
    Miserable wind,
    You beg it
    To stop.

THE HEAVY WEIGHT

I have so much
    Compassion
    For those who have
Stepped over the line.
The way back
Is ten times the way
There.
That first step
Is so easy.
You get what you crave,
What you want,
What you think you
Deserve.
Then,
Arriving
At the center of the
Labyrinth,
Reaching the turning point,
The hard stop,
Then the clawing back,

Each inch a torture,
Back to the integral
You.
Still tempted,
But not vulnerable,
Learning
The stop sign of life,
And the yield sign
When needed.
My muddy boot
One step at a time,
Never going back,
But seeing those not yet
At the center,
Or never will be.
The path is still
The becoming,
Always available
But seldom chosen.
That nudge
Can be taken
Or ignored,
A little blur
At the edge of your mind.

COURAGE STEW

Take one pound
    Of fear.
    Two pounds of sheer terror.
One drop of hesitation.
Three pounds of
Leap of faith.
Three pounds of
Trust yourself.
Four pounds of
Step into the unknown.
Mix together
With a few drops of forgiveness.
Eat heartily,
And watch the outcome
Unfold.
Repeat anytime.

COLD FEET

In the long dark months
    When the cold
    Never leaves my feet,
I remember
The hot exploding
Feeling
Of the sun on my ankles.
Then feeling 10 times
Their size
But looking normal.
I let them burn
Knowing
The coming cold,
The heavy socks,
And boots
None of which ever
Causes the sizzle
Of now.
I risk the burn
In case it deepens

Into my bones
But it doesn't.
We have to be
In the now,
However ghastly despicable.
Find a way to love
Where we are.
There must be a pink cloud.
Find the crack,
The nugget,
The reason
That comes out of struggle
And sacrifice.
That's the beauty
Of warm feet.
They will tell you where to walk.

LESSON 101

What is a mistake?
    A tear in the skin of time?
    A regret with an excuse?
Please forgive me
I say to myself,
As the shame deepens
My face.
You don't get a do-over.
Or do you?
You did what you thought best.
Or what you wanted.
All of it turns to the dark side,
The path to the left,
The woods,
Exciting,
And enticing.
Just a little way
And then head over heels.
You must extricate
Yourself.

You knew.
Does that make it worse?
Now you can get off your high-horse,
Rub your eyes,
And make amends,
By forgiving
Everyone
Human,
Including yourself.
And maybe it was all
Exactly
How it was meant
To be.

FRIEND

The webs
    Of our two lives
    Criss-cross
Unexpectedly.
A recognition
Lights up life.
Suddenly hopeful,
Energized,
Spirit to spirit.
We are not alone.
I know you,
Stranger.
And you know
Me
In the deepest way.
Sharing love,
And joy of life,
Blooming,
Lotus-like,
On the water's surface

However murky within.
Not by chance this meeting,
This stunning realization,
And the unbearable gratitude
It brings
At the perfect design of the creation
We call our universe.
This cross-path not random,
And the kickback is
The little piece of knowing
That,
From the vast and powerful,
incomprehensible,
Largely unfathomable,
Beyond.

LEAP OF FAITH

Those hard choices
    Build up,
    And form the background
For the next hard leap.
A parka in winter,
Insulating from
The dread of winter,
Or the gaping unknown.
Just a step over the bridge
Into the sea.
It will cradle you
And wash you.
Fear has evaporated with the mist,
And the luxuriating swim
Is the reward.
Take it.
It's yours.
You earned every bit of it.

SPITTING IMAGE

I looked in the mirror
    And a stranger looked back.
    It was shocking,
But vaguely familiar.
Out of the past,
My grandmother stared at me,
Equally startled.
I felt a wave of shame
At the wrinkles and gray hair.
Then I remembered
My grandmother died at 56.
I am 77.

THE GIFT

What a miracle is
    Pen, Ink,
       And paper.
Words form language,
Image and symbols,
The weaving of thoughts
They create
Safer than memory,
Their letters
Making a remembrance
To return to
When sadness envelops
Or inspiration has dried,
And blown to dust.
Read again,
And feel mere words
Dance into sunlight,
The dust now sparkling,
The warm blanket now circling,

Soothing,
Making everything
New again,
And perfectly
All right.

BOMB CYCLONE

The gloom
     Slowly became dark,
     The gray sky
And dropping snow,
Now invisible.
I'm wrapped in my shawl,
Not even
Too warm.
Writing in the dark
Again.
The silence
Is singing a bright hum
In my ears.
The absence,
The void,
Of the people I love,
Is haunting me.
The open space
In front of my heart,
Just a vacuum

Pulling on the strings,
Dragging them near,
As if to comfort,
And surround me.
In the deepening night,
They fly elsewhere,
Cease to exist for me.
And I'm left
With a taste of connection,
Now only an aftertaste.
Not long lasting
But enough
To bring a memory
Of times not alone,
But not fully felt,
Or lived.
It seemed so ordinary,
Then.

KUPUNA

I no longer have dreams.
    I can only have regrets.
    Putting on the brakes,
Feet digging in,
As I slide toward
The river's edge.
Perhaps time left
Will stretch
To allow
Twists and turns
Of remnants
Unfulfilled,
The cream of life
Turning.
I have no breath
For newness,
No strength
To fight for rising,
But I can gently rest,
And digest

The hairpin turns
Of the journey traveled.
No trophy,
But no graveside prayer
Either.
There is still
A bit of challenge,
Fresh,
Yet to be discovered,
To be lived
Equally alive,
And full of sweetness.
The last breath
Not taken,
Yet.

IT'S A SHAME

I'm bleeding
      A thousand cuts.
      Each,
Small and deep.
None is lethal
By itself.
The blood runs
To heal the shame
Of some unknown
Transgression,
A perfect flaw,
Now,
Retreating,
Into the darkness.
To be healed
Alone,
And without scrutiny,
Lest,
A worse fault
Be discovered.

And shame
Upon
Shame
Hiding
Behind the rock walls
Of granite
And cold steel.
Resolving
To be unknown,
Out of sight,
Buried so deep,
As to be
Invisible.
It is a secret
Who I am.
Maybe always.

THE SUCCULENT

Plants sleep,
    Too.
        In the night,
They don't need to move.
In the day,
They are slaves
To the sun's force,
Bending and swaying,
Lunching on the sweet rays.
In the dark,
They rest.
Whispering to each other,
Sending signals,
Wishing for roots
To entwine,
Sharing secrets
In a language
Unspoken
By mortal beings.
Their ears are tiny

But powerful,
Witnessing
The cry,
The anger,
Or the soft breath
That brings the gentle water.
Awake and aware,
They take your poisons,
And give back
Vitality,
Elixir,
That your cells crave.
They will heal you
If you let them.
And smile
If you thank them.

CHARGING STATION

I feel the body
    Electric.
    My electrons
Are charging.
Trapped in their circles,
Endless in their orbits,
Trying to escape
But held firm
In the grid of
Connection.
Humming,
And exchanging energy
For all my parts,
Even my brain.
Needing the spark,
The fizz and snap
That makes life
Zing.
My hands burn,
My head buzzes.

I follow all your paths
At once,
To the sudden opening of
Time and space.
The vision
New and bright
That carries me into an ocean
Of awareness.
So tenuous
It's almost out of reach,
The dream,
Half remembered,
Fading before me,
Needing the lightening bolt
Of recharge
That is inspiration.

CHATTERBOX

My inner voice
    Is quiet.
        The small, small,
Honey drip
Of words
Is empty,
Right in the center
Of the plus minus
Magnetic poles.
How exhilarating,
To be at nowhere,
With no push or pull,
Just soft smile,
Rest.
The layers of the onion
Peeled,
The core
Sweet and devoured.
Now,
The sound after the bell

is rung,
The incense burned away,
Nothing left,
But a pinpoint
Of potential,

Resting on the surface
    Without ripples,
    Without movement
    Or plan,
    Floating
    In the vast ocean
    Of the hauntingly,
    Endless,
    Universes.

THE WEDDING

I am marrying
    My mirror.
       You reflect back to me
All the things
I don't want to see,
My shame,
My anger,
My not goodness.
And I reflect back to you
Anything hidden
Inside.
Pain and denial
Are the order of the day.
It is a thankless task,
And the hardest
Of hard
To be a companion
Willing to endure
The slings and arrows.
But the noblest effort

To trust each other
With honesty needed,
To improve the worst of you,
Becoming better
In body, mind, and soul.
Don't be tempted to escape
The hard, hard.
The reward is beyond
Priceless.
Bow down and honor
The strength needed
To polish the mirror.

YIN YANG

Welded
Melded
Joined
Connected
Intertwined
Collected
Together
Inseparable
Combined
Wedded
Yolked
Mixed up
Coupled
Mated
Fused
Paired
United
Bonded
Tied
Blended

Shared
Stuck
Glued
Harmonized
On the same page
I got you
Besties
We are one.

MOLECULAR

I am connected to
    Every quark
    That exists,
Near or far.
Distance is not real.
It is a crackle glaze
That connects
Everything.
I am all,
And all is me.
There is just one
Me,
And it's really
Big.
I am natural
Because
I exist in a natural
Universe,
A giant organism
With organs of galaxies,

And a brain
That is a black hole,
Or a worm hole
To multiple dimensions,
Happily spinning,
As if invisible,
And hidden,
With a smile,
For the undaunted
Explorer,
Driven to take
The treacherous voyage
To understand
The heart of all
That is.

TRUTH SERUM

I can't unsee
    What I've seen.
    Or not know,
What I now know.
It's a photo,
Snapped,
In my mind,
Present after every blink.
Heart stopping,
Stomach sinking,
The real, real.
It changes
Everything.
That truth
Washing over me
To a hard stop
At my lowest level.
The movie keeps
Playing,
But without the wool

Pulled over.
Feeling
The worst
Of human
Emotions.
The deception,
The lies,
Not confronted,
But known from
The inside out.
I shall not
Remain
Silent.

BIRTHDAY

My planet
    Went round
    The same star
78 times.
Do I remember
Any of them?
Not distinctly.
Should I ?

MY TEETH FALL OUT.
    My bones soften.
    My hair grays.
    But still,
    I persist.
    Not done yet.
    What meaning
    Lies ahead
    In the next
    Go round?

All that went before,
Waiting ,
For a single moment,
A nidus of meaning.

Up ahead
Is unkown,
And the go behind,
A blurry collection
Of jumbled images.
It's purpose
Will become clear,
And I'll know
The satisfaction.
Just like the last piece
Of the puzzle
Placed.

LIAR, LIAR

Oh, the people
    Who have lied
    To me,
Greedily stolen
From me,
All the while
Grinning wildly.
I can't touch them,
Now.

But the heart anger
    Needs it's own
    Revenge.
    Smoothe it
    Like a trowel
    On fresh cement.
    Burn it
    In the fiery furnace.
    What remains,

The great forces
Will take
For the perfect
Justice
To be meted out,
Dispassionately.
This time,
Forgiveness
Won't help them.
Their fate is set.
Mine,
Yet,
To be determined.

HALEAKALA

I imagine
    The dry windswept
    Cauldron.
I taste the bitter
Burnt dust.
No life forms
Seen.
Exquisite cold,
Reddish soil,
Swirling
About the footsteps.
Then,
The profound sense
Of primitive
Raw explosions,
Making a land
That didn't exist.
I feel the frightening
Of what lies beneath.
Feeling naively safe,

But knowing the
Crackling force,
Smoldering,
Waiting patiently,
For the perfect time
To become alive,
To become the God
That rages,
Takes the power,
The creator/destroyer.
I am the putty
In the hands
Of the ultimate
Furnace.
I dreamed of this
Fiery life/death
That transforms
Everything
From nothing
To something.
I am not spared.

THE HEREAFTER

How it was
     Before the future
     Happened.
The not knowing place,
That feels so safe,
So now.
Not thinking
Of the ahead,
How it would be,
After,
Everything changed
Again.
I'm happy now,
Forgetting
It will never be
Like this forever.
The string
Will fray apart,
Threads flying,
Unraveled,

Broken
Into brittle bits,
Too small to be glued,
Only memories
Intact.
I did not cherish
The time,
Taste it,
As delicious nectar,
Precious and rare,
Until gone.
The painful
Look back,
Don't go there,
Or to the ahead.
Feel deeply,
And stay
Here.
Now that you
Know.

FOREST TREE

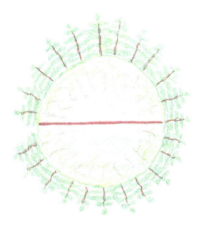

WHO?

Beyond the needs
    Of you,
        Is where I will go
To find out
Who you are.
Not the sucking,
Hungry,
Cold,
Tantrumed,
Or else,
Self.
But into the core
Of warm honey,
Crackle fire,
Laughing,
Ladling soup,
Herb friendly,
Goodness.
Inviting,
Frolicking,

Beckoning,
Without the bitterness
That lays
On the outside,
Sticky and stiff,
Not brushed off,
But crushing
The goodness
Into a nut.
Which can
If soil given,
Reach to a tender stem,
Then a sheltering
Home,
Trunk wrinkled,
And textured.
I will tap that syrup
Until it runs
Freely,
The taste rich and sweet.
Until,
I'm satisfied.

I HATE YOU

Anger is a seed.
　　　Don't plant it,
　　　Or cultivate it.
If it grows,
It turns bitter,
And poisonous,
Paralyzing,
Lethal,
And murderous.
Let it dry,
And wither.
Find the tree or vine
That grew that pod.
Who picked it?
An impulse,
Or a mistake?
It can be dug up,
But its roots run deep,
Its seeds many.
Dig them up.

Smash them.
Burn them.
Chop the roots.
Plant some sweet smelling,
Fragrant,
Something,
That will quiet the harsh words,
And bring a smile
To the most ugly
Of faces.
Even yours.

ECLIPSE RETURNED

Sadness,
    Is the shadow
    Falling as the earth
Turns.
An emptiness,
Hollow,
Missing
What was once there
Or never was,
But always
Wanted.
It fills the body parts
With longing.
My hands ache,
Magnets,
For the unknown.
To fill the void,
Lest it crumble,
And collapse,
And the dust escape.

It can be tricked
Or distracted,
But not for long.
And not just anything
Will do.
I'll wait,
Until the sun returns.
Will it be enough?
Or will that hollow
Echo
Remain
To beg
With tears borrowed
From past memories,
Veiled,
And buried deep
But never
Really
Forgotten.

THE CLIMBER'S DILEMMA

I live in the crack
  Between the worlds,
  A climber suspended.
One foot on each rocky
Wall,
Trusting the shoes,
And the stone,
Will hold and
Guide me.
Perhaps,
A passing bird
Will drop some nourishment.
Do I try up
Or down?
Once the crevasse
Has widened,
I need to choose
A side.
That changes everything
Forever.

The path,
Uncertain,
And unknown,
Guaranteed
Rough.
Eyes up
Not down.
The fall long and hard,
If one foot
Slips.

STONEY CREEK

There is a cave
    Inside my heart,
    Or my body.
It's been growing
Stalactites
And stalagmites
For a long time,
Trying to knit together
Into a solid stone.
The river running through it
Is a renegade,
Its source
Unstoppable.
No slow drip,
But a mighty wave
Raging havoc
On any harsh
Stony madness.
The rock will surrender
To the torrent

In time.
Meanwhile,
As it carves
Deeper,
More room
For
Laughing water.
Til no stone
Is left untouched
And no thought
Is left
As is.

FINALLY

I breathed in the cold,
    Nose and lips tingling.
    Air,
From a frozen
Arctic place,
Half a continent
Away.
Bird songs
Defy the chill.
Sun weakly warming
Where the wind
Isn't.
Plants so long
Asleep
Desperate
For a green shoot
To start.
Wary of the cold.
It's a slow start.
Taking any chance

With a bit of warm,
To press those buds,
Lacy and red,
Roots still shivering.
Tiny flies
Are lazy
In the sunlight,
As if
It is summer,
Unperturbed,
By the chill wind
That makes even
Deep throated birds
Struggle
To sing their arias.
The audience
Hunched over
In their long cloaks
Hurries home,
Heads covered,
Waiting for the
Wind
To change direction
From the arctic
To the tropic,
And then
Everything
Will come
Alive.

GEN?

It got dark,
    And life passed.
    The trees suddenly
Towering,
My grandchildren
Grown.
Voices deep,
And chins strong.
I lost them
To their own space
Unreachable now.
I am on the other side
As if already
Passed,
A spectator
Across the growing
Canyon
That separates
The young
From the old.

Hoping
That the spirited ones
Will rope up,
Climb hard,
And reach the heart
Of those
That love them
Most.

SUSPENDED ANIMATION

After the rain stops,
    The water becomes
    A colorless gray,
The same shade
As the sky.
Separated,
By a line of trees,
They seem
The same essence,
Flat and lifeless.
Only tiny ripples
Mar the surface,
Marking it as liquid,
And not air.
The moment ,
Suspended,
The pause before the breath,
Waiting for movement
Or color.
Anything,

Other than the unreal
Stillness.
Anticipating
The crashing down
Of chaos,
Of life,
In its full intensity.
The pause interrupted
By the train starting up,
Gaining momentum,
Until there is no longer
The in-between,
And the measured breath
And stillness
Is only a memory
Fading,
As the train speeds away.

THE LONGEST DAY OF THE YEAR

I waited so hard
    For the day.
    It came and went.
Now I'm chasing the other side.
After the fullness passes,
The emptiness starts to grow,
Draining me
In a thousand cuts,
Seeping out slowly.
What's left is
Shriveled,
Deflated,
Hallow,
Sadness.
The sun dims,
The earth grows cold.
There is only tiresome waiting,
The expanding so slow
I'm put to sleep.
The glorious longest

Day,
Out of reach.
I love that fleeting moment.
Someone show me
How to love the wait.

DOG DAZE

Don't just use 'em up,
    Those days of summer.
    There is an end.
You'll know it
Like a slap,
When it comes.
So don't wait for that.
Sit in the heat of it.
Feel your skin sizzle.
Sweat if you want.
Let your cold bones
Unbend.
And,
Moment by moment,
Breath by breath,
Inhale
All of it,
Until your lungs
Almost burst.

The exhale
Is going to take a lot longer.

WHAT WAS I THINKING?

THE GOLD DIGGER

Searching for that glint,
    Covered in mud.
    Digging out
That solid beauty
Inside.
Seduced by the lure
Of uncovering the precious,
That's what drives the work
Of mining.
Makes one able
To crouch in a cold stream,
Legs giving way,
For the glint of a flake
That suggests
More to come.
It's not greed,
But lust for perfection,
And disgust for the dusty.
Throw it in the crucible

Of ordinary life,
And reveal the gold.
I knew it was there
All along.

THE MIDNIGHT SUN

Even the endless
    Sunset,
        Of the arctic circle
Still ends.
The darkness descends,
But not fully.
Torn clouds
Teasing,
Streaks of orange-red
Remain.
But the wait is over.
The night is done.
The earth turns,
And my turn is done.
Adventures still await,
But after that,
It's time to be tucked in,
To rest,
And enjoy the big sleep,
Watching the reel of past times

Flash past.
A gentle smile
Forgives
The past misadventures,
And then,
An embrace
Of what comes
With the wake up
In a new place.

ALEKSANTERI

I sat in your birthplace
    And your father's birthplace.
    What was it like
Being you,
When you were were young?
I only knew you
When you were old.
Hearing aid,
Insulin shots,
And a fat belly lap.
We didn't know a word
Together.
But I sat on your lap and laughed.
Twenty years old,
You left your family
On a ship
Across the ocean.
It cost forty dollars.
But the cost was infinite.
You never saw them

Again,
Except for the ones that ventured
With you.
Your sisters
Big and tall,
Never found peace.
Your brothers scattered everywhere.
Your fate
To dig in the mine
Year after year.
But you escaped
Serving
In the Russian army,
And not to die
In a faraway place
For someone's idea.
I'm glad you came
On that ship
And had one boy
Amid six girls.
He was my father.
No more
Need be said.

ALEKSANTERI REVISTED

I'm not done with you
    Yet.
        Your memories
Are in my DNA.
That's why I wept
When I saw the road
To the farm.
My going in,
Your last look.
I know now,
Why you had a cow
In your garage.
You played there,
And grew there.
I feel your hopes,
And fears,
Your sadness,
And resignation.
Did you love the one
You lost?

Or the one you got?
After forty years
Not a word of English.
I wish you could
Know me.
But then in a sense
You are me.

METSA (FINNISH FOR FOREST)

I'm emptying myself
  Into the earth.
  My bare feet
Are planted on the ground.
Above me
Different birds cry,
The sun slanting,
But warmth not gone.
A soft breeze
Makes a sound
I can't describe.
It is leaves rattling,
But more than that,
A tapering,
Swirl of sound
That becomes my breath.
The forest behind me
Has a sound, too,
A lively hum.
Mixed with birds and wind,

It becomes a symphony.
Am I conducting?
Or composing?
I am the one concert goer
Today.
And it's always a different score.
After I leave the stage,
Someone will sit
Where I sat,
Baton in hand,
And the music will go on.

WE USED TO

We used to have bats.
They don't come
Anymore.
But mosquitoes still do.
We used to have clams.
They don't come anymore,
Either.
Now we have zebra mussels.
Things
Disappear so fast now.
And new things,
Aggressive and invasive
Tip my world over.
No checks and balances,
Nothing to rely on.
Oh yes,
My hair turned gray.
But I expected that.
I didn't expect
The bats to disappear

Or the unpredictable
To make me scared.
All you new invaders,
Don't get too smug.
What's to come
Is patiently waiting,
Poised to take you over.
Maybe no one else will notice,
But I'm watching.

REALLY?

SUPER BLUE MOON

I hear the sound
    Of September.
    The crickets are more intense,
Louder,
And insistent,
The tempo faster,
Reaching a crescendo.
The low, big moon
Feels ominous.
Something is about to happen.
The smell is different,
Damper,
Earthier,
And a chill comes
Into my breath,
Unexpectedly.
The warm
Is seeping away.
Not yet cold,
But suggesting

That the earth,
Tipsy,
From all that steamy heat,
Just might need
To take a rest,
And the big chill
Will soon
Overtake us,
However fast
We try to run away.

SLEEPING IN

In-between
    The Dreamtime
    And awake time,
Floating back and forth,
Over here,
Over there.
You are almost awake.
Shut your eyes,
Don't move,
Drift back,
And watch it.
It feels so buoyant,
So liquid,
So peaceful,
Magically unhurried.
I could suspend here,
Forever,
Between the real,
And the unreal,

And have the best of both worlds.
But one world
Is calling louder.

TOENAIL MOON

Waning
Comes every month.
Whether you feel it
Or not.
The shining toenail
Shrinks smaller
Until black.
The end of frivolous
Or important,
A door closed on a painful
Wound.
Round the bend
Is the excitement
Of beginning,
Waiting for swelling,
Full tummy,
Fat brightness.
Plenty of moons.
To luxuriate in.

Just remember,
There's not always
Plenty of moons
Left for you.

JUST A FEW QUESTIONS TO KEEP IN MIND

Did the Buddha hurry?
    Or did he just go faster?

Will a tree keep growing taller?
    Or will it just get fatter like a human would?

Can you dare to love yourself?
    Can you feel you deserve love?
    Can you feel you are loved?
    Can you feel you are love?

Do you think you can bargain with God?
    It doesn't work.
    You just end up bargaining with yourself.

Do you remind yourself constantly of your dharma?
    Do you know your job is to make the world a better place by changing yourself?
    By searching out the origins of judgement and fanning

compassion, by understanding the influences that create nasty people. Nothing matters but to cultivate love for everything and everyone. That is your dharma.

Do you want wisdom or joy? If you choose wisdom, it turns out to be joy. If you choose joy, it turns out to be wisdom.

DEDICATION

To my lovely grandfather Aleksanteri, and his beloved Lapland. His courage, determination and gentle goodness inspired and pushed me to go through rough and hard times and delight in the beautiful times. Carry on all you beautiful descendants and know he's chuckling and smiling at all of you.

ALSO BY KRISTIN KESKEY

Falling Into the Ocean

Writing in the Dark

Ghostriders

Blown Out of Orbit

The Bear and the Raven

Available on Amazon or through my website: www.kristinkeskey.com

ABOUT THE AUTHOR

ABOUT THE AUTHOR

Writing passionately, and from the heart, I am an artist and MD specializing in nutrition and obesity. Believing in the path to self betterment and making the world a better place, I've encountered many speed bumps along the way including losing the sight in my right eye. My poems and drawings have created self-love and healing for me, and I hope for you, too. I have 4 children and 6 grandchildren and live in Michigan. I invite you to please join my email list to receive updates on my next books and more.

For more books and updates visit:
    www.kristinkeskey.com

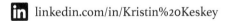 linkedin.com/in/Kristin%20Keskey

Milton Keynes UK
Ingram Content Group UK Ltd.
UKHW020622151223
434433UK00009B/33